Quick Money in a Weekend

QUICK MONEY ON A WEEKEND

By: D.K. Hawkins
Series "Quick Money"
Version 1.1 ~November 2022
Published by D.K. Hawkins at KDP
Copyright ©2022 by D.K. Hawkins. All rights reserved.

No part of this publication may be reproduced, distributed, or transmitted in any form or by any means including photocopying, recording, or other electronic or mechanical methods or by any information storage or retrieval system without the prior written permission of the publishers, except in the case of very brief quotations embodied in critical reviews and certain other noncommercial uses permitted by copyright law.

All rights reserved, including the right of reproduction in whole or in part in any form.

All information in this book has been carefully researched and checked for factual accuracy. However, the author and publisher make no warranty, express or implied, that the information contained herein is appropriate for every individual, situation, or purpose and assume no responsibility for errors or omissions.

The reader assumes the risk and full responsibility for all actions. The author will not be held responsible for any loss or damage, whether consequential, incidental, special or otherwise, that may result from the information presented in this book.

All images are free for use or purchased from stock photo sites or royalty-free for commercial use. I have relied on my own observations as well as many different sources for this book, and I have done my best to check facts and give credit where it is due. In the event that any material is used without proper permission, please contact me so that the oversight can be corrected.

The information provided in this book is for informational purposes only and is not intended to be a source of advice or credit analysis with respect to the material presented. The information and/or documents contained in this book do not constitute legal or financial advice and should never be used without first consulting with a financial professional to determine what may be best for your individual needs.

The publisher and the author do not make any guarantee or other promise as to any results that may be obtained from using the content of this book. You should never make any investment decision without first consulting with your own financial advisor and conducting your own research and due diligence. To the maximum extent permitted by law, the publisher and the author disclaim any and all liability in the event any information, commentary, analysis, opinions, advice, and/or recommendations contained in this book prove to be inaccurate, incomplete, or unreliable or result in any investment or other losses.

Content contained or made available through this book is not intended to and does not constitute legal advice or investment advice, and no attorney-client relationship is formed. The publisher and the author are providing this book and its contents on an "as is" basis. Your use of the information in this book is at your own risk.

TABLE OF CONTENTS

Quick Money in a Weekend 1
TABLE OF CONTENTS 4
INTRODUCTION 6
CHAPTER 1: WHY MAKE QUICK MONEY ON A WEEKEND? 9
CHAPTER 2: WAYS OF MAKING QUICK WEEKEND MONEY 12
   1. Selling Other People's Stuff. 12
   2. Writing Articles. 14
   3. Create a blog. 20
   4. Home caretaker. 28
   5. Housekeeping services. 35
   6. Residential painting services. 39
   7. Dog walking services. 42
   8. Vending Machine Business. 46
   9. eBay & Craigslist. 50
   10. Swap Meets Marketing. 52
   11. Babysitting. 61
   12. Sell Supper. 64
   13. Paid Survey. 64
   14. Sell Space For Advertising On Your Blog. 66
   15. Affiliate marketing. 67
   16. Online auctioneer. 70
   17. Freelancing. 71

18. Receive Cash for Your Electronics. 72

19. Work in Auto Detailing. 73

20. Cake Sculpting. 73

21. Animal Photography. 74

22. Custom-made things. 74

23. Tutoring. 75

24. Vehicle Detailing. 77

25. Commercial Property Preservation. 78

26. LifeGuard. 78

27. Stagehand for a band or theatre group. 79

28. Start A Car Servicing Business. 79

29. Participate in a bottle drive. 79

30. Hold a yard sale. 80

31. The Newsprint. 80

32. Temporary Landscaper. 81

33. Start A Small Business. 81

34. Utilize Your Know-How. 81

35. Private Vacation Rental. 82

CHAPTER 5: COLLEGE STUDENTS' FAVORITE WEEKEND JOBS. ...85

CHAPTER 6: EARN $1,000 IN JUST ONE WEEKEND. 88

CHAPTER 7: STEPS TO FIND A WEEKEND JOB QUICKLY. 94

CHAPTER 8; MY TOP 50 WAYS TO MAKE $100 ONLINE ON A WEEKEND. 98

CONCLUSION. 106

INTRODUCTION.

This weekend, there are many opportunities to make a quick income without spending a thing. Certainly, there are many different cost-free alternatives to earn money. Many individuals have mastered these methods and have begun to leave the rat race gradually. Permit me to provide some simple techniques for escaping the rat race.

For instance, obtaining reprint articles is the quickest way to get started with AdSense blogging. Reprinted articles are free articles that can be posted on a site as content. You would first sign up for a free blog and post your reprint articles there.

Then, publish at least 10 posts and submit them to the leading directories to promote your site, and voila! People will become interested in your blog and will undoubtedly click on your AdSense advertisements, and you will be compensated for this so that you will have some quick cash before the weekend! (The answer to making large amounts of money with these blogs is to create at least five of them.)

Getting started with article distribution to article directories may not earn you much money immediately. Still, this process builds steadily and makes tremendous amounts of traffic when you submit many articles.

There are various methods for joining forums and selling content. You will be astonished by how many individuals wish to purchase your stuff. I've done this, and people adore purchasing forum content. How much can you earn simply by creating and selling articles?

If you are serious, you can write an article in fifteen minutes and charge $5 for every article. You can see how quickly this will accumulate and earn you at least $100 by this weekend. Here are some of the best suggestions for crafting, but here is the final solution.

Currently, if you believe that your wage is sufficient, you are mistaken. People compete to find more employment to improve their financial situation for a brighter tomorrow. Weekend part-time employment is one of the most common extra jobs.

Its sole purpose is to boost your financial well-being. Also, flexible hours will benefit others and won't interfere with your primary employment. If you decide to hunt for weekend employment, the explanation below may be of assistance. Happy Reading

CHAPTER 1: WHY MAKE QUICK MONEY ON A WEEKEND?

First, we need opportunity, which the modern economy provides daily close to where you reside! For most families that live paycheck to paycheck, it is a blessing and still extremely possible to earn quick cash every weekend. I am not referring to multi-level marketing, product creation, or cold calling.

It is difficult when you are doing everything you can to pay your bills, and a small increase in income would provide you some breathing room. Once I discovered this, I could pay off my car and credit cards with the other cash generated. They were my primary concern because I was weary of paying all my money to creditors but if you want a large-screen television, go ahead.

When I describe a single method for earning money quickly, I am not referring to free money that can be gotten without effort, as this doesn't exist. If you don't mind a little legwork, you can establish your own business for less than $100 and operate under the radar while generating extra income. then, attentively listen.

Whether the economy is strong or bad, everyone's priorities shift, and the same is true for those who store their most prized possessions in small storage units. Some of these units are eventually abandoned, and the monthly rent isn't paid. This is an excellent opportunity to bid on a unit and win its contents.

When you win an auction and explore the compact storage unit's contents, it is like Christmas. Some products, like the high-end video camera I won, will be useful to you and your family. Then you will need to get prices for the other things, which I will show you how to accomplish easily online.

You don't need to sell these products; simply submit an advertisement with the appropriate language to make it stand out. In addition, there is a website that can sell your goods in less than twenty-four hours for cash at no expense.

Examine the mini storage units in your neighborhood and adjacent municipalities that you can use to earn quick cash. The contents of these Storage Units must be relocated before they may be rented out again. You offer a service to assist them, for which you are compensated generously.

More than ninety percent of those who read this will do nothing. Those who will now put in a bid may be deterred by not winning bids the first time and abandon their efforts.

You, however, are not like them; you need this and are persistent; you realize that over time you will learn new things by speaking with those who have previously earned experience and achieved great success.

CHAPTER 2: WAYS OF MAKING QUICK WEEKEND MONEY.

1. Selling Other People's Stuff.

Helping others make money is a lucrative business, and there is a strong possibility of giving others a quick and easy way to earn money. Most of us have accumulated more material possessions than we need. This is a golden opportunity to acquire a business that would prosper during economic hardship.

How? You can make money on the weekends by giving your services as a Garage and Estate Sale Planner and selling other people's belongings. We already know that many people have many items in their garages or homes that they may sell, and we also know that people are attempting to save money so that they will purchase at discount stores. What could be a better shopping venue than a garage or estate sale?

You offer to organize the sale of items from A to Z so that people can arrive with a tidy sum of money at the weekend. You will be responsible for each aspect of the project. You compose a list of the products to sell and the price to sell them for and simply have your client sign the form and give them a copy. You will arrange the advertising and promoting of the sale and even the selling of the products themselves.

You could be astonished to realize how much people truly have to sell and how much worth that lies awaiting in a garage. You can also alert neighbors that you are conducting a sale and ask if they want to organize one.

They can participate by preparing a box of products for you to pick up. This could lead to another client desiring their sale or simply giving them a taste of what you are doing for their neighbors. In either case, you are assisting those in need of a little other cash and gaining a business that needs just your talent to organize and advertise.

2. Writing Articles.

Are you aware that writing articles can provide substantial income? It is regarded as one of the internet's increasingly multibillion-dollar industries. What are the keys to being a successful article writer or operating a home-based business that sells article writing services? I will describe the seven habits of a successful article writer.

Proactive.

When starting a business, you will discover that thousands of others do the same thing, but why do some people excel while others fail? Unsuccessful article writers passively anticipate an order. This characteristic distinguishes good article writers from others.

They don't invest time in developing their article-writing business. One can be proactive in many ways, including creating a video profile, attending article writing courses, and networking with other authors online or offline. All these actions will make more article writing orders and suggestions on becoming a better writer.

Long-term perspective.

Successful article writers have a long-term goal that will lead to long-term success. They establish their lifestyle objectives so that they can work whenever and wherever they choose.

With this lifestyle ideal in mind, they would do all possible to achieve success. As with all other internet businesses, article writing isn't a quick way to earn money. It takes time to develop expertise, reputation, and SEO.

Being Punctual.

Who's got the time? No one is correct. Successful article writers understand the importance of punctuality. They establish daily, hourly and second-by-second objectives to work on.

This is how modest effort accumulates success over time. Delivering high-quality, on-time content to your customer would improve your reputation. It becomes a free internet advertisement for you.

Always Victorious.

Successful article writers don't seek win-lose circumstances in business transactions. They will concentrate on how their job can assist others in generating revenue. They share their contacts and resources with other article writers to establish a large network. Thus, a sustainable business may be created by utilizing their knowledge and skills to attract many prospects.

Be Positive.

The principle of the Law of Attraction is effective for article writers and their businesses. Positive energy draws positive energy to itself. They find ways to improve when they are confident in their work and accept responsibility for the outcome. Therefore, they rapidly expand their network.

Be willing to learn.

Knowledge is constantly evolving. Article writers can choose niches with more expertise but must continually refresh their knowledge, terminology, and expressions. No matter how polished their talents are, their writings will fail to captivate readers if they cease to learn. If you write like a professor from the 1980s, it will be impossible to attract readers.

Commitment.

This is an essential habit of all successful individuals. Delete "I will try" from your mental dictionary. When they transform "trying" into "must," they commit. This will involve giving up their free time to watch endless soap operas, Facebook, and window shop on weekends. When they encounter barriers or rejections, they immediately recall their vision and resume work.

You can't wait to begin writing, so you should connect with an article-writing specialist who can serve as your mentor. The first step is for him to share his years of experience and a secret library. Click here for further details.

Article marketing is a simple way to make money if done correctly. It is easier than many other online moneymaking opportunities. For example, marketing using articles is much simpler than search engine optimization, in which you attempt to rank pages on your website for various keyword phrases that a user may enter into Google.

Videos are the only thing I can think of comparable to articles, and video marketing is practically the same as article marketing, except you use videos. This marketing is also significantly more forgiving than pay-per-click marketing, where you might quickly lose a lot of money. It also needs far less time than social media marketing.

You can make huge money with article marketing! It's basic. You are not required to create an elaborate website or anything similar. To start, you only need a computer and some sitting time. Oh yes, you must know what you're doing! In light of this, let's examine some of the talents you can need for success in this form of marketing.

Well, what can I say? You must have the ability to write. You are fortunate, however. This isn't school, and you won't be graded. Actually, they will assess you by purchasing your goods, but this isn't a traditional grading system.

If you can write, you can make money with article marketing; but you don't need to write effectively. The fact that you have meaningful content in your writing is vastly more essential. It doesn't need to be earth-shattering.

You don't need to find Einstein's formula every time you write, but you must be able to convey knowledge that others need and want. This indicates that you should likely write articles on perpetually popular topics, such as weight loss, self-help, and how to make more money.

3. Create a blog.

You've probably heard that blogging may be lucrative, and you've probably been inundated with email pitches touting how to make thousands overnight by writing alone. Who couldn't use extra cash every month in these challenging economic times? Fortunately, you recognize a scam when you see one and have not fallen into the marketers' trap of purchasing program after program in search of one that works.

The true tragedy is that you can make money blogging, and thousands of people are already doing so. You won't become wealthy overnight, but if you're prepared to put in a little effort, you may make a steady income to assist with family needs. If you commit the time and effort, you can make millions (but not overnight). You could replace your day job with a blog.

But to make money, you must understand the fundamentals of the blogging industry.

Pick A Niche.

You will need a topic to write about; selecting the right one can mean distinguishing between success and failure. The ultimate goal is to attract visitors to your website, cultivate a relationship with them, and then sell them something. Choosing a niche with little competition is crucial to reaching this objective.

How do you accomplish this?

There are, nevertheless, certain general guidelines to keep in mind. An old direct marketing proverb is that a marketer (which you will become) must identify a hungry crowd, determine what they are hungry for, and then feed them.

Another criterion is locating an audience whose demand occupies their thoughts at least once per day and in which they have an emotional investment. For instance, a person with hypertension presumably considers it daily when they take their medication. They are emotionally invested since they may die from this sickness. They are desperate for a cure or, at the very least, relief from the adverse effects of the medication.

These audiences are abundant in niches addressing health, relationships, or wealth.

Locating a crowd is simple. Finding an audience that is starving for something needs more effort.

One method to determine what this demographic is craving is to observe what they are purchasing. This can be done online by visiting Amazon and examining the best-selling products in a given category.

Or, you can leverage the tens of thousands of dollars others have spent on market research to determine what they are offering. A visit to the website for "Dummies" books, for instance, will provide you with a list of the titles they sell. These titles would not be offered if they were not selling.

Once you've chosen a niche, you should attempt to make it as specific as possible. For instance, if you choose trading stocks, you may refine your focus to day trading futures.

Focusing on day trading futures eliminates a substantial amount of competition and speaks to a niche clientele. In addition, the keyword term "day trading futures" receives approximately 9000 monthly searches.

Select A Product.

After selecting a niche, the next step is to sell something, which is the simple part. Every manufacturer sells through affiliates, including Wal-Mart, Macy's, and tens of thousands of others.

You could search Google for products linked to day trading using the preceding example by typing "day trading affiliate." Choose three or four and register. You'll receive some garbage, but you'll also acquire some jewels.

Your Blog.

There are many free blogging platforms, such as Blogspot.com, Weebley.com, and 2.0 networks, such as HubSpot, Squidoo, and many others. However, if you wish to monetize your blog, you should get your domain name and host it yourself.

There are two primary justifications for this little investment. First and foremost, it is your website, and anyone else's terms and conditions do not bind you. You can do anything you like with your domain without fear of being reprimanded. If they determine that your specialty is spamming, they may close your blog if hosted on a free domain.

Secondly, the domain name itself is essential for effective SEO. Using the example of day trading, you might attempt to acquire daytradingfutures.com, .org, or .net.

Content Is king.

Even if you have the hottest niche and the most popular product, you will fail if your content lacks value. Do not post meaningless content just to post something. The text must be grammatically sound and either instruct or amuse the reader. If you struggle with writing, you should contract it out. A variety of freelance writing websites offer qualified writers at reasonable rates.

Take Steps.

Once this site is up and running, you must continue to provide great content; this is one of the benefits of using the free blogging platform WordPress for your blog. If you spend a weekend writing 15 or 20 blog posts, you can load them into WordPress and schedule them to be published over a specific period. This creates the sense of "natural" growth, which Google loves, and gives you a nearly three-week respite from writing.

You may be somewhat dismayed to discover that it is not always as simple as people make it; many people who tell you it is simply are attempting to take your money. There will be simple and difficult approaches to doing a task like anything.

Doing things the difficult way might result in frustration and eventual abandonment of an endeavor.

One of the reasons why making money with blog websites is simple is because they enable anyone to post content to the Internet rapidly. This is true for those who have been working online for an extended period and for technophobes.

Most current blog software is free and stupidly simple to install and manage. Following basic instructions will enable you to begin making money with blog websites almost immediately, even though there is a slight learning curve associated with working in this manner on the Internet.

You will first need to set up your blog. This can be accomplished in several ways, either by creating a free blog website or, for a more professional approach, by purchasing a domain and hosting. If your goal is to earn a couple of dollars, you may be able to do it without paying money at websites such as blogger.com.

However, if you want to create a business and generate long-term income from blog websites, you may wish to adopt a more professional appearance.

Although a great deal is involved in launching a business of this nature, it need not be too complicated. There are many outstanding manuals available that will walk you through each stage of the procedure. By carefully following these steps, you may have everything set up and begin earning money from blog websites within a weekend or two.

Most successful blogs begin as weekend hobbies that later bloom into businesses. Examples of a food blog are KampungboyCitygal.com, which covers the Asian cuisine scene. The New York Times has covered their blog and recently added a section about their trips.

If you are skilled at writing and have enough content to last for three to six months, you can make a sustainable quantity of blog traffic and interest. Once you have a certain amount of traffic, you can expand your blog by seeking guest bloggers or reviewing articles from other bloggers.

Successful bloggers can make cash by advertising on their sites or publishing product reviews that their readers may find useful. In addition, their blogs may garner a significant audience, resulting in a lucrative book contract with a prominent publisher.

4. Home caretaker.

Many people are radically altering their life to become full-time caretakers of estates, farms, ranches, or even nature preserves. The caregiving profession has existed for millennia and is not new.

However, the modern era has provided us with the choice of air travel and the opportunity to communicate through the Internet and newspapers. These two venues have brought caregiving as an opportunity for everyone to the forefront.

Many situations necessitate the services of a caretaker, the most common being the purchase of a second or even third residence owing to a job. Parents are no longer leaving their children with a nanny or relative when they travel; instead, they are bringing them along.

This has motivated many individuals to purchase a second home. These individuals are unwilling to rent out their second property. They desire the ability to return at any time.

Others are purchasing second homes in popular holiday destinations. These individuals are not interested in simple real estate investment. This vacation property is purchased to provide an open invitation to family and friends who may wish to visit at any time.

People are living longer than before, which is a well-known fact. A working farm, ranch, or inn owner may hire a younger worker to assist with property management. Their adult children may have their occupations or may not wish to play such an active role in running the family business.

It is known that second-home insurance premiums are greater than those for a primary residence. This increase is attributable to insurance firms' awareness that second homes are typically vacant. The likelihood of a break-in, flood, or fire is increased in these residences. These groups are discovering that employing a caretaker meets their various demands.

Engaging a caretaker can marginally reduce insurance rates depending on the insurance company.

Those who employ caretakers also discover that it saves them money over time. Having someone on-site to perform routine maintenance, identify possible issues, and make repairs as they emerge is considerably more cost-effective than hiring outside help for a major undertaking.

Also, their homes and possessions are secured from potential burglaries, vagrants, and board youngsters who may choose to loiter. Caretakers might be recruited on a short- or long-term basis.

Individuals or families who provide caretaking services are seeking a change of pace. Typically, they are city inhabitants wishing for a change in atmosphere and way of life for their families and themselves.

Some individuals would never work with animals or in a wildlife preserve. Some may not be able to migrate to remote or rural places. The vocation of caregiving provides doors for them.

Typically, caretakers are retirees. The urge to feel helpful, the desire for a second profession, and the chance to get lost in a new environment attract retirees to caregiving. Their prior life experiences will serve them well as they enter the caregiving sector.

Employment as a caretaker is guaranteed to anyone skilled in land management, gardening, maintenance, and animal care. Caretaking at a hostel or inn could be a viable alternative for someone with experience in delegation, management, and customer service.

In recent years, it would have been impossible for retirees to follow their goals and relocate to a chosen region. However, this is no longer the case. Those who have always desired to cultivate their land, work with animals, or reside on an exotic beach might achieve these goals through caretaking.

Young families are also finding employment opportunities as caregivers. Many major property owners, ranchers, and nature reserves employ parents of small children to assist with site maintenance. Parents choose to relocate to teach their children different parts of the world and new ways of life or get them out of the city and closer to nature.

An essential aspect of understanding caregiving is that it is a leisure activity. It is not like the business world, and you do not have to worry about living under the surveillance of a dictatorial employer.

Most owners are not even there, and those who understand the value of solitude and a tranquil environment are. The setting allows the caretakers to travel at their own pace and enjoy all of its perks.

Free rent is the primary perk granted to caretakers. This will allow retirees to save, pay for their children's education, or cover other household expenses. Free-rent also aids young families who are saving for their own homes. In this laid-back environment, caregivers must be highly independent, self-motivated, and capable of working independently.

Depending on the employment, a small stipend or pay may be provided, as well as health insurance. The caretaker typically covers moving charges, but the owner may occasionally cover these costs.

The responsibilities of a caregiver will vary depending on their location.

However, the top priorities of all caretakers are integrity and a passion for the environment. Working on a horse farm, working ranch, or nature reserve needs a passion for animals.

Hostel or inn caretakers must have a passion for people and customer service. Depending on the caretaker's interests and areas of competence, a suitable owner can typically be identified.

Most property owners are willing to train an individual with whom they have a relationship, who they view as trustworthy, and who has potential. Owners would prefer hiring someone they believe to be trustworthy than someone with a page of references whom they suspect may be a crook. It is also crucial to remember that individuals who do not consider themselves experienced in specific areas might gain a career as a caregiver.

Caregiving is an excellent method for retirees to spend their golden years. Together, the leisurely, relaxing pace, natural surroundings, and free accommodation provide a life-changing experience, unlike anything they have ever had. Caretaking is also suitable for opening their ranch, inn, or fishery.

It affords students the chance to learn while saving money. Families benefit from rural environments and the capacity to instill a passion for the land and animals in children. The money saved on housing can be invested in a future home or their children's education.

The caretaking arrangement benefits both the owner and the caretaker. Reports reveal that there are a rising need for\scaretakers around the world. Establishing a good link between the owner and the caretaker is possible. The Internet and newspapers can be used to locate owners and caretakers.

If you can demonstrate that you are a reliable home sitter, this is a great opportunity to earn money and save on rent. This possibility is most effective during the summer when people travel for extended periods and need someone to look after their property or pets.

A friend of mine does this as a summer job during college. In addition to earning money from house-watching throughout the summer, he also saved money on rent for his college accommodation.

5. Housekeeping services.

Nowadays, housekeeping services are extremely popular. As people become increasingly busy, they need individuals who can take care of their houses; therefore, professional home cleaning is a fantastic method to earn money in the modern era. The best aspect is that you will need minimal financial investment; all you need are housekeeping abilities and a lot of hard effort.

Before starting, ensure that you have the necessary equipment. First, you will need cleaning supplies. Consider reputable, efficient brands that can complete the task with little effort.

Next, gather all the necessary cleaning supplies. Some customers bring their cleaning products, while others want you to do so. In either case, it is preferable to have all bases covered. Moreover, make sure you have access to transportation.

Once you are prepared to launch your professional cleaning company, you can begin marketing your services. One of the best ways to start is by utilizing your network. Ask your acquaintances whether they are interested in your services. You might offer them cheaper pricing and request that they refer you to their other acquaintances. In the end, word of mouth is a tremendous marketing instrument.

To broaden your audience, you will need Internet access and a computer. Marketing your professional cleaning services online is a fantastic strategy to reach customers directly and to make it easy for prospective clients to contact you. The Internet is overflowing with demands you can fulfill, so you won't have to exert additional marketing work after you've spread the word.

The disadvantage of Internet advertising is that you may receive consumers in remote regions, which you may not be prepared to drive to. Consequently, if you wish to keep your business local, at least for the time being, you can employ more conventional marketing strategies, such as printing fliers and business cards. If you are willing to spend a little money, you can advertise in the local newspaper.

As your clientele expands, you may consider bringing a partner to your professional cleaning firm. A partner will expedite the cleaning process and allow you to schedule additional clients. Having a companion also increases your safety.

After all, when you spend a reasonable amount of time in a stranger's home, there is always the possibility that harmful scenarios may arise. You should always have a mobile phone if you cannot find somebody to assist you.

Cleaning services are an excellent weekend business to launch. Most individuals working all week hate cleaning and packing their homes. Here, you can earn extra money by performing little tasks such as laundry and basic cleaning services. You can charge by the hour or provide weekly cleaning services in bundles.

For instance, you can charge $xx per hour for house cleaning services. You can get paid in advance if the client commits to four monthly cleaning services. In addition, you might receive a referral fee for basic maintenance services if the home you are cleaning also needs services like carpet shampooing or plumbing.

6. Residential painting services.

One of the advantages of running a painting company is the flexibility it can provide. It is feasible to work only three to four days per week and earn between $50,000 and $600,000 per year, given the high revenue potential.

Painting houses is one of the few recession-proof businesses that may put financial security within reach for many people. There are no formal schooling requirements, and only fundamental painting and business abilities are required for success. (Most of which can be learned with the proper home study course on developing a painting business.)

Typically, a home painter needs relatively minimal physical labor, which can be performed by men, women, and individuals of any age. Painting can be employed as a full-time or part-time source of income.

In addition to the ability to swiftly make a professional income, owning a painting business gives the satisfaction and pride that come with being self-employed and independent. Not to mention the instant joy you receive each time you complete a work, add another delighted customer to your list, and deposit a hefty check into your ever-growing bank account. It's a pleasant gig!

Spend some time acquiring information from trustworthy sources about promoting your painting business and bidding and estimating paint projects, or what I call the "business side" of the painting business.

New painting business owners regularly ask me, "What types of jobs should I pursue?" This is a marketing-related inquiry. My response is consistently the same. Start by seeking home painting projects. They are abundant and the simplest tasks to paint, offering tremendous profit margins and little overhead costs.

The residential re-painting market is unquenchable; there is sufficient work in this section of the painting industry to keep painters busy and profitable for life.

Another amazing advantage that makes starting a painting business appealing is that you do not need a significant initial investment. One of the most widespread myths about expanding a lucrative painting business is that you must invest thousands of dollars in advertising to get customers.

You may build a flourishing painting business based only on referrals with almost no traditional promotion. This is not true, especially if you are focusing on residential touch-ups. Even someone starting from scratch may get their painting business up and running and produce money in seven days or less on a budget as low as $250.00 with some simple procedures.

These are a few reasons why establishing a painting business piques the interest of so many individuals and why it consistently ranks among the greatest small businesses to launch.

If you have a paintbrush and a free weekend, you can start a house painting service for the elderly or real estate agents who wish to spruce up their clients' homes before selling them. You never realize how much more authority you can command by just repainting a room.

This is a simple yet effective company that you can start by posting flyers in your neighborhood or contacting real estate agents whose contact information may be published alongside their properties for sale if they need painters to spruce up their property before presenting it to potential buyers.

7. Dog walking services.

A dog walking business can be an enjoyable and lucrative way to earn money at home. A professional dog walker walks clients' dogs regularly, alone or in groups. There is a growing demand for these services because many families have busy schedules and cannot exercise their dogs because they are away all day. Exercise is crucial to proper pet care, and many pet owners rely on dog walkers for assistance.

There are many benefits to starting a dog-walking business. Genuine affection for dogs and the physical stamina to walk the dogs are the only abilities required. Commitment and dependability to your dog walking regimen are crucial. You can find lots of information about dog care and canine behavior in books or on related websites available at your local library.

Your startup expenses are modest. You may need to acquire many high-quality leashes, excrement scoopers, and bags. Purchasing liability insurance is usually recommended. Also, you may maintain your health and fitness while earning money! With a dog walking service, your operating costs will be low, and the profit potential is high.

Before starting this home-based business, you must arrange a few details. You must plan your daily itineraries and walks. Determine the finest places to walk the dogs and map out thirty-minute itineraries. You must establish your fees. Find out what other dog-walking firms in your area are charging for their services.

Choose the type of dog walks you will provide, such as private or group walks, the number of walks per week, etc. If you are just starting, you can gain relevant experience by volunteering to walk dogs at local animal shelters and dog rescue organizations. This will offer you experience handling a variety of dogs and give you the confidence and credibility to obtain dog-walking jobs that pay.

Finding dog walking jobs with a little marketing and advertising budget is possible. Designing and printing eye-catching and informative flyers is a cost-effective method for advertising your pet services. Distribute these leaflets across your community to attract new customers.

Post posters in office buildings and retirement communities to reach the busy professionals and seniors who are likely to hire a dog walker. Vacationing pet owners frequently need the services of a dog walker. Post your flyers on community bulletin boards.

Veterinary offices, pet grooming services, and pet supply stores are other helpful locations for posting flyers. If you provide an excellent and dependable service, you will be astounded by the number of referrals you receive after gaining your first customers.

This is a great place to work if you enjoy dogs and are punctual. You might begin by posting posters on the community bulletin board or asking neighbors and friends for referrals. For example, if you walk a dog for $x, you could inquire whether the owners would allow you to walk their other dog simultaneously.

You can fast double your revenue in this manner. You can add extra income streams to this business by obtaining referrals for pet care services or writing articles for magazines catering to pet owners for a nominal price.

The first step to a successful business is to take action and get started. We have given you five ideas this weekend to stimulate your interest and get you moving.

8. Vending Machine Business.

Ah! The business of vending machines! What attracts individuals to it? Certainly, money is to be made, and the fact that it is a cash-only business makes it much more attractive. I imply that no invoices will be sent to companies. Simply refill your machines and withdraw the cash!

There are some considerations to make before plunging in, even though it sounds and is, in fact, fantastic. One thing to remember is that it is a business that needs some effort and ability.

Work and expertise go hand in hand. It is simple to refill a soda machine. After doing anything a few times, it becomes simple, but what about identifying places for your vending machine placement?

This is the aspect of skill I was referring to! It needs patience and perseverance to locate the venues and clinch the sale. There is a procedure that occurs from the time you meet or contact your prospect until the time you install your machines.

This transformation doesn't occur overnight! It could take a week or many months to finish. It depends mostly on the timeframe in which your prospects intend to deploy your vending machines.

But if you adhere to your prospect like glue, continue to follow up with them, and ensure they have the information they need from you, you will close more sales than you can imagine!

Can you find a solution to their dilemma?

Can you do anything differently than everyone else? Before purchasing a vending machine, conduct essential research. You will avoid many headaches along the road.

This business can help you achieve independence if you start correctly. So read everything you can and conduct as much research as possible before going in headfirst!

Some individuals have fallen victim to con artists that wish to offer you overpriced machines and take your hard-earned cash. Please don't be fooled!

Find a trustworthy distributor of vending machines in your area and purchase from them before buying units at a seminar. Start by building one machine at a time and learning as you go.

If you are not purchasing an established vending route, developing your business will take some time.

What if I told you that if you persisted and devoted yourself to expanding your vending business one machine at a time, you might earn more than you do at your full-time job?

Permit me to share a little story.

I was employed as a city bus driver full-time when I entered this industry. As he was transitioning into a new field of work, a coworker of mine requested

I assume responsibility for reloading the office soda machine.

I immediately noticed that I was earning $75 to $100 per week by selling a few cases of soda consistently. This piqued my interest! Therefore, I contacted a vending machine distributor that could sell me machines.

This is where everything began for me when I started working part-time. I went from business to business, knocking on doors and requesting permission to install a soda machine.

Since we already have machines, I must admit that I received some negative responses. However, and this is a Major But! A few individuals along the way answered yes! So, as I moved from place to location, I gradually expanded my business one machine at a time.

As word spread that I was in business, I began to receive references along the way. Then I began to push my business to the next level by reinvesting my profits and advertising to my target demographic.

That was when things began to take form! When you can market to your prospect, so they contact you first, you will close more transactions, obtain more business and earn more money.

So how did I accomplish this?

With hard work, perseverance, and an "I won't quit" mindset, I was able to accomplish this. I will tell you that studying and investigating this company beforehand helped me succeed.

9. eBay & Craigslist.

Initially, eBay and Craigslist were excellent resources for obtaining instant income. Over three million individuals rely on eBay as their primary source of income and primary supply of merchandise. Some individuals earn extra money by purchasing things from these websites and reselling them at a greater price. Why wouldn't you investigate this option?

A website is also an automatic cash machine! As of January, I saw this endeavor as "out of my league." I was so incorrect! Anyone may make a website and start earning money within hours! This concept should not intimidate you. It is easy to construct your website.

Finally, if you don't like to develop your website, many individuals are prepared to pay you to market theirs! If you don't know this, use any search engine to look up "affiliate marketing" to learn more. This business can make up to a thousand dollars weekly with no startup fees. The secret is discovering a program that pays to depend on a percentage of sales.

There are some low-paying schemes but also programs that pay many hundred dollars for each sale. Before you sign up for any affiliate program, you need only examine the compensation structure and determine if it is worthwhile to promote. This will provide you the opportunity to build the high-profit business you desire. Spend a day investigating this possibility.

10. Swap Meets Marketing.

There are regularly scheduled Flea Markets and Swap Meets in cities and towns of all sizes across the country, each of which attracts hundreds, if not thousands, of bargain hunters.

They may be held in the local drive-in theater, in huge parking lots, warehouses, parks, or community centers - anywhere with sufficient space to set up booths and attract an audience.

Most of the time, these competitions are held on weekends, although in other regions, they can begin on Thursday and last for four days. Swap meetings and flea markets are entertaining, lucrative, and a terrific way to establish a business. Many individuals who started with Swap Meet sales have gone on to build Gift Shops or Mail Order enterprises of considerable scale.

According to the FAR HORIZONS Business Coaching team, three unique varieties of swap meets exist.

Note: (For the sake of simplicity, from this point on, when we refer to "Swap Meets," we also mean flea markets, craft fairs, and similar events, as explained below.)

1. Outdoor Swap Meets.

In terms of merchandise, these are typically diverse. You can discover anything from high-end stereo systems to designer jewelry to families cleaning out Aunt Emma's garage of old tools, toys, and other parts and pieces. Typically, these events attract individuals seeking substantial discounts and deals.

2. Indoor "Malls."

These typically attract a more experienced type of marketer. The exhibits tend to be more ordered in appearance, and the quality of the merchandise is often higher throughout the entire event. There may be booths instead of tables, and each marketer prefers to specialize in particular product areas.

3. Craft Shows.

These may be held indoors or outdoors, as part of a local carnival or in parks, fund-raising events, county fairs, or other events of a similar nature. Typically, vendors display their items from booths and depending on the region. The options might range from homemade to expensive (or homemade and expensive).

Don't forget this when packing for the swap meet.

Over the years, dozens of successful Swap Meet vendors have told us that the two most essential things you can bring with you are:

1. An optimistic disposition.

2. A disposition to negotiate and "play the game."

One member comments, "People come to Swap Meets hoping for a deal and go because it's enjoyable. So I maintain a positive attitude and am always willing to negotiate.

I have bottom-line pricing in mind and never go below it, but I'm always prepared to negotiate a bit on the original asking amount. Thus, my buyer is satisfied with the purchase, and I maintain a healthy profit margin. We both benefit."

Regardless of the type of Swap Meet, you choose to organize initially. You must do a few simple, fundamental steps before, during, and after the event.

Let us begin with. Well, this is the start!

HERE ARE A FEW THINGS TO DO BEFORE STARTING.

1. If you don't already know, find out where the local swap meets are. This should not be too difficult, as they advertise in local newspapers and free

publications in convenience shop racks. Smaller meets may not advertise, but you should be able to find them by contacting nearby drive-ins or rummaging through the telephone book.

2. Next, personally scout the competition. Observe the tables and booths from the perspective of a marketer. What do the merchants carry? More significantly, what do they not have? What are their prices?

3. Book a table (or booth, as the case may be). Contact the meet manager; he or she will supply you with price information and a list of the rules and restrictions you must adhere to when marketing at the meet.

Depending on the meet, the cost of renting space at a Swap Meet ranges from a few dollars per day to much more. Try to begin at a low-cost, well-attended meet to minimize your initial financial outlay.

4. Select your desired items. The Business Coaching staff at FAR HORIZONS typically suggests starting with $450 to $750 worth of merchandise (meaning your actual cost).

5. Prepare your other supplies.

You can need to bring all or any of the following, depending on the event:

1. Minimum of one folding table.

2. A cash box contains dollars and change.

3. Foldable chairs

4. A pristine tablecloth.

5. A huge umbrella, tarp, or other sun protection for your customers (and yourself).

6. Some transparent plastic to shield your items from precipitation (obviously, this applies to outdoor meets).

7. A Yellow Price List so you determine the bottom line when it is time to negotiate.

8. Many business cards.

9. Some catalogs, brochures, New Arrivals flyers, or other promotional materials to help increase sales.

10. A customer order book that allows you to write receipts and record customers' names, addresses, and phone numbers.

11. A calculator.

12. A rubber stamp for endorsing checks.

IMPORTANT.

Do everything possible to collect lots of information as possible about each consumer. In addition to the name, address, and phone number, try to obtain the customer's email address, fax number, and credit card information, provided you have a merchant account.

THE BIG DAY ARRIVES.

If you are well-prepared, the day of the competition should proceed rather well. Sure, you'll have lots of work to do, but you'll also have fun - especially when you start making sales and earning money!

Here's what you must do on your first day at a swap meet:

1. Turn off the alarm, wake up, shower, and get moving (we did say this was a step-by-step instruction, right?).

2. When you arrive at the gathering, locate your spot and set it up. Your program video provides instances of the proper and improper display. Rehearse your set-up at home to plan the most visually appealing exhibit before arriving at the convention.

3. Determine your "bottom line" or the lowest acceptable price for each item. Our Business Coaching staff suggests 1.5 times your cost as a good rule of thumb.

4. Prepare to accept checks. Verify the current address and phone number and if possible, include a driver's license or identification number on the check. Many consumers will prefer this payment method, and vendors report a negligible number of "bad" checks.

5. Every customer's name, phone number, fax number, and email address (as many of these as possible) should be recorded.

6. You can need a partner to help run the cash register while you handle sales.

There are a few essential tasks to complete after one Swap Meet concludes and before the next one begins.

1. Create your mailing list by adding all collected consumer names to your mailing list. These will become an integral element of your follow-up marketing activities over time.

2. Plan/implement mailings - Based on the size of your list, you will need to begin sending follow-up mailings to your clients.

This covers the fundamentals of Swap Meet Marketing, but the most important thing is enjoying yourself. Many sellers like to involve their families (including their children) and spend valuable time working toward a common goal on the weekends.

Swap Meet marketing is entertaining, rewarding and can be accomplished with only a few hours per week of effort. A handful of sellers mix business with fun by traveling from Swap Meet to Swap Meet around the country. They use the profits from each weekend to fund their travel and purchase other products for the next meet!

11. Babysitting.

As a mother, everyone needs a day away from their children and the demands of daily life; therefore, you can capitalize on other mothers' desire for time alone. Don't believe for one second that you are alone, as you are not. Many mothers can't stand their children; if this describes you, you can be just what they're searching for.

Mall-based babysitting can be both entertaining and lucrative. Sometimes, busy shoppers tire of dragging their children from store to store. And sometimes, all the children desire is a brief nap.

If you have experience babysitting or have operated a daycare, you might have fun and make easy money by caring for children while their parents shop at the mall. All you need to do is approach the mall services; there are almost always empty stores, and the mall has excellent security.

The store may easily install monitors to assure the safety and security of the children. They can also arrange for a security officer to be present for you.

They'll be thrilled to be able to persuade parents to shop, and you'll have a good time and make easy money watching children.

Children are tired of being taken to the store, hungry, and irritable. A safe and secure location for parents to leave their children while they shop would be a wonderful comfort.

Produce a copy. When parents drop off their child, make a copy of their driver's license, and when they return to pick up their child, need them to present the original. This will safeguard you and the shopping center.

If the shopping center installs cameras in the store, no one can accuse you of wrongdoing. The children have a pleasant respite. And you earn money while having fun.

Try what I did if you need money immediately or within the hour. I am making more money today than I did in my previous business, and you can, too, if you click the link below and read the incredible true tale. I was suspicious for only ten seconds after joining before I knew what this was. You will also be beaming from ear to ear, as I was.

12. Sell Supper.

This may necessitate permission, but it's not a big deal. Every mother knows that the weekend is her time off from cooking; therefore, you must prepare and deliver meals to the families you have lined up.

On a regular weekend, you could earn many hundred dollars in profit, and the greatest thing is that you never had to leave your home but for the delivery portion.

13. Paid Survey.

An online weekend job can help you earn $200 or more without ever leaving your home. The nicest aspect is that there is no interview procedure or such bullshit. You simply work as much as you like, and the money you make is transferred into your account as soon as the work is complete.

Many individuals who have discovered that they enjoy the extra money from an online weekend job now discover that they make more than at their regular employment. With just a couple of hours on the weekend, earning another $250 or more is feasible. If you consistently do this on Saturdays and Sundays, you'll have an extra $2,000 at the end of the month to help pay bills or enjoy yourself.

However, you should watch out for businesses that try to persuade you to pay money to make money. Don't be fooled by this. Legitimate weekend job websites don't charge a fee. They should compensate you.

Paid survey sites are among the most flexible and popular online weekend job sites. Many businesses and industries always attempt to obtain client feedback, yet it is too costly to conduct extensive market research initiatives. Therefore, they pay individuals $5 to $50 to conduct an internet survey.

Because they only take 5 to 15 minutes to complete, it is simple to complete a large number of surveys in a single day, which is why people can earn over $250 per day simply by sharing their opinion.

Signing up for a free paid survey site, searching the database for the highest-paying surveys, and completing the form are the only requirements. Once you click the submit button, your earnings will be transferred immediately to your bank account or PayPal account.

14. Sell Space For Advertising On Your Blog.

If you have a website or blog, you can make other cash by selling advertising space on it. This weekend, you can apply many internet advertising networks to place their advertisements on your website.

Google AdSense is one of the most prominent advertising networks. After submitting an application and having your website approved, you will receive a code to copy and paste to display relevant content advertisements.

You will earn money when a visitor clicks on an advertisement. Other advertising networks to which you can apply include Chitika and TextLinkAds. Simply conduct a Google search for more advertising networks.

In addition, if you already distribute a newsletter to your readers regularly, you can make other revenue by selling sponsorships or advertising space on your newsletters. For instance, if your newsletters are on dog training, you can approach a local or online pet store for sponsorship in exchange for an advertisement in your newsletter.

15. Affiliate marketing.

Have you ever wondered how to make money quickly using affiliate marketing? Today marks the end of it. In this essay, I will define affiliate marketing and explain how to get the maximum money from it.

After learning my secret strategies and understanding how to make money with affiliate marketing, I can guarantee that you will never again seek a regular job. Because being an affiliate is so advantageous, and you may select when to work and when to take days off.

Imagine you work four hours per day, as I do use a computer and an Internet connection. You can work from any location on earth!

How does this affiliate program function?

As an affiliate, you are essentially the business owner, but you are not required to develop, store, or ship any products. The firm supplying the affiliate program handles everything else. You need not even be concerned about customer service, as every strong network already has that in place.

Therefore, your sole responsibility is to make targeted visitors to the affiliate offers. If you have been attempting internet marketing, you will find it quite simple. It is not particularly difficult.

You can perform this action if you've ever recommended something to a friend, perhaps a restaurant or film to see. The only difference is that you will be compensated for each reference you make.

A few easy steps are required to make money as an affiliate:

You must first choose the product you wish to promote. After that, you must develop an offer. Start with free web publishing tools such as Squidoo or Blogger. They are extremely user-friendly and rank extremely well in search engines.

After you're done, you may begin promoting your Squidoo page using article marketing, video marketing, social bookmarking, and other techniques.

Once these promotion strategies are launched online, you may anticipate a certain amount of traffic to your free offer websites. Now is the time to unwind and let the internet make some money for you.

I believe there is nothing simpler to learn than generating income with affiliate marketing. Therefore, you have nothing to lose by attempting the endeavor.

Many huge organizations are eager to write substantial checks to individuals who successfully promote their products or services. If you have used or purchased internet items or services before and can testify to their quality, you can earn a substantial income online.

You receive compensation when people click on your links and make a purchase. Author Rosalind Gardner is one of the successful affiliate marketers who switched to full-time internet business. Her book, "Make a Fortune Promoting Other People's Stuff Online," is titled "Make Huge Income Promoting Other People's Stuff Online." She consistently earns six figures online from home.

16. Online auctioneer.

You can auction off items you've made yourself, such as Christmas candles or homemade soaps. Other items you can resell online for a profit include inexpensive items to add value. For instance, if you have located inexpensive origami paper, you can include an eBook on origami designs and auction the paper and eBook on sites like eBay.

If you are successful as an auctioneer, you can function as a "trade assistance" for others who wish to sell their sites. In this manner, you can earn other revenue online in addition to your auction earnings.

Starting a weekend business won't interfere with the lifestyles of most individuals and may lead to larger earnings in the future. In addition to boosting your income, you can gain vital business skills through a weekend business.

17. Freelancing.

Companies of all types need writers but often prefer to outsource the work rather than pay the high costs associated with hiring a full-time staff. The Internet is an excellent resource for finding this type of work.

The funny thing is, you don't need to be a skilled writer. If you can write coherent sentences and conduct a little research, you can often complete a freelance writing project without difficulty if you possess these skills. Have some writing or funny experience? Even better.

Regardless of your skill level, weekend employment options are available. Perform an online search for "freelance writing jobs.

18. Receive Cash for Your Electronics.

Eliminate all your outdated cell phones, digital cameras, laptops, MP3 players, movies, and camcorders. They are wanted by a firm named Gazelle, which will even pay for shipment.

I discovered an amazing fact on their website: they pay their customers an average of $115. This is a wonderful weekend cash bonus for the duration it takes to find and pack your belongings.

19. Work in Auto Detailing.

Auto detailing may be the perfect year-round weekend job for you if you want to earn other money on the weekends and enjoy working on automobiles.

It can be relatively affordable to launch an auto detailing business, and it can also be lucrative. You can have reliable and consistent side employment with just a few frequent paying customers. If you enjoy working on automobiles, you cannot even consider this activity "work."

You should educate yourself on the subject if you are unfamiliar with detailed work. Visit your local bookstore or library and check out some auto detailing manuals or enroll in a class - you can search online for colleges.

20. Cake Sculpting.

Starting your cake-decorating business can be much fun if you can bake and are creative. If you have a creative flair, you will attract clients who want your one-of-a-kind cakes (that they can not get anywhere else). People tend to spend more money on others than on themselves, and distinctive things that many people can enjoy typically make more revenue.

21. Animal Photography.

Photography is a lucrative industry, and pet photography is a specialized specialty that eliminates a substantial amount of competition. If you have some camera skills and a little imagination, you can be astonished by the success of this "small business concept." I recently read an article about a successful "niche" photographer who photographed sleeping infants exclusively.

Create a simple website and upload examples of your "pet photography" work so potential clients can see what you do. Remember that pet owners adore their pets; having a snapshot of a pet with its owner is wonderful. A unique birthday present, Christmas cards, and even a pet photo calendar might be created.

22. Custom-made things.

There are internet stores where you can offer custom-made things. They provide the products, while you provide the design. You are not required to purchase products in advance or pay for a website.

Customers visit these websites (such as Cafe Press) to purchase goods. When a buyer orders a product bearing your design, the company distributes the goods to the customer and gives you a percentage of the profits.

Be careful that your weekend labor doesn't become too lucrative. You can need to quit your job and start a business doing what you love.

23. Tutoring.

With the current economic climate, many individuals find it difficult to meet ends. To afford the goods we need, many of us must acquire a second job or a weekend job, even though we are employed.

There are simple part-time weekend occupations that anyone may perform. This page will outline some accessible employment opportunities.

Fundraising for a nonprofit organization is a worthwhile, well-paying part-time employment. People with strong communication and marketing skills can begin working as part-time fundraisers. You can earn money while also assisting those in need. The primary objective here is to solicit charitable contributions from individuals.

A tutoring business is another excellent option to earn extra money. This part-time employment is advantageous in that it is straightforward to obtain clients. You can approach the local school or ask parents whether they would allow their child to receive tutoring in a certain subject.

After a period, you will acquire other consumers because parents and children won't notify others in need about your service. Therefore, you won't need to advertise if you perform well.

There is no requirement to leave the house. Online activities for which you are compensated are another excellent option to earn money on weekends. One of the most popular in this area is paid surveys.

After registering, you can connect to the survey site to complete the surveys. This simple task you can perform in the evenings after your 9-to-5 job, allowing you to earn more money. You can make substantial extra money each month depending on your investment time.

24. Vehicle Detailing.

This type of work is likely the easiest and most flexible for you. It has been classified as a job with a remuneration sufficient that approximately $250 per car is earned (around 4 hours).

You begin by placing pamphlets under the windshield wipers of filthy but considered expensive automobiles. Moreover, if you need a new brush, pail, and rags, you can issue capital for less than $50.

25. Commercial Property Preservation.

If you enjoy working outside, this job is ideal for you. Many significant corporations seek employees with this experience. The pay for this position is pretty high. In addition to reasonable compensation, you also receive free exercise and fresh air.

26. LifeGuard.

Most weekend jobs pay very low. Typically, lifeguards are compensated at the rate of a regular civil employee in the city or town where they work, which is higher than the minimum wage. Imagine how fantastic your physique will be! You can learn if you don't know how to swim.

If you've always wanted to become a lifeguard, decide to make it your backup source of income if you already have a job. The exercise will be fantastic, you'll have free access to the facilities, and you'll be able to spend hours doing worthwhile, gratifying work. If you are a student, the pay is excellent, and what an asset this reference will be to your resume in the future.

27. Stagehand for a band or theatre group.

Many establishments offer a flat rate for each engagement, regardless of the number of hours or the weekend length. This may not appeal to a 40-year-old instructor who dislikes rock music but not all music is rock.

Suppose you are a child and manage to become a roadie for a rock band; kudos to you! Some symphonies use part-time support on weekends when their regulars are off. Sometimes, theater companies employ assistants with the same wage scale.

28. Start A Car Servicing Business.

Most individuals possess automobiles. Utilize their asset by offering to wash, vacuum, and clean the entire vehicle. You can charge more when you combine services (washing, vacuuming, window cleaning, etc.).

29. Participate in a bottle drive.

Grab your pickup and collect unwanted bottles door to door. Many individuals recycle; however, many lack time to transport their recyclables to the bottle shop. Offer to do it for them and retain the results for yourself. This can add up to a substantial amount of money in recyclable goods.

30. Hold a yard sale.

Now is the ideal opportunity to sell unwanted items and eliminate clutter. Simply place an ad in the local newspaper, distribute fliers, and organize your yard sale.

31. The Newsprint.

The delivery of newspapers is yet another viable way to earn extra cash over the weekend. You could make a little bit of money by investing more time and energy. You could contact your local newspaper distributor to inquire about weekend delivery availability.

32. Temporary Landscaper.

If you have a knack for landscaping and design and can freshen up lawns, a position as a landscaper would be ideal for you. Landscaping includes planting trees and flowers, laying sod, and designing gardens.

33. Start A Small Business.

You can create a small business that runs solely on the weekends or part-time. The enterprise could range from producing pastries for special occasions to window washing. Window washers earn an hourly wage. To start a window washing business, you should target businesses that need the service on the weekend, such as restaurants and houses.

34. Utilize Your Know-How.

Utilize your information effectively. Are you an effective math educator? You have the option to become a math instructor. You might offer your services as an editor or tutor if you are proficient in English. Make your skills work for you.

In addition to the possibilities listed above, you can try something creative and entertaining to earn money on the weekends. You might organize church or local community flea markets or assist in setting up fairs and indoor malls. Many buyers attend these fairs, and you are certain to locate some devoted customers.

35. Private Vacation Rental.

Long-term luxury vacations are available to individuals who can afford private vacation rentals. Depending on the duration of their trip, temporary tenants typically occupy these properties for one to two weeks.

The houses are completely furnished with standard furnishings, and private vacation homes typically include private hot tubs or pools and exceptional views. If you possess properties that can be converted into holiday rentals, you should consider renting them out privately.

First, determine whether your properties meet the requirements for personal vacation rentals. These homes should be strategically positioned near commercial centers, restaurants, and tourist attractions.

The proximity of your houses to golf courses, beaches, ski resorts, or the mountains will be an additional selling advantage.

Determine if there is a market for categorized vacations before starting the refurbishment process. You will need a high demand and a limited quantity of private vacation homes in the area surrounding your properties.

Obtain the essential legal documentation for holiday houses. Renovate and furnish your homes to make them as comfortable as possible. Luxury private holiday homes must include a stove, fireplace, and swimming pool.

Include images and a detailed description of your properties in your listing. Include all the available activities and public amenities in the neighborhood's list. You can put your listing on free websites online, utilize rental companies, or, if necessary, create your website.

At this level, vacation rental software is useful because it assists with handling reservations and properties. You can run the business independently or engage a team to assist you with managing rental accounts, providing housekeeping services, performing maintenance, and advertising private vacation rentals. You might also offer free and simple packages to attract travelers.

CHAPTER 5: COLLEGE STUDENTS' FAVORITE WEEKEND JOBS.

To prepare for their future careers, college students no longer waste their free time on online games, chatting, and other frivolous activities. They begin searching for weekend employment opportunities to increase their income. The top three weekend occupations that they prefer are mentioned below.

Tutor.

This position is ideal for college students. It doesn't need a high level of manual dexterity. While revising prior information, you might make more revenue. Compared to other jobs, this position is comfortable and well-paid.

Not only may it improve your speech expressiveness and endurance, but it can help consolidate your knowledge. Most importantly, your working hours are nearly weekends or extracurricular hours. Therefore, it will never hinder academic pursuits.

Attendant or waiter.

It has been popular to seek part-time employment in fast food restaurants like KFC and McDonald's. They often hire temporary staff on weekends and holidays. Due to the hourly wage and shift work pattern, you can only work on weekends. This weekend job isn't particularly taxing, but you must provide courteous customer service and be able to handle unexpected situations.

Internship.

Internships can benefit the future careers of students. Students can suggest themselves if they have demonstrated expertise in their majors. However, your internship may occasionally be unpaid. Different employers will compensate you differently.

Ultimately, your most important asset will be your professional experience and excellent practical and hands-on skills. Companies, supermarkets, hospitals, and public institutions typically give internship opportunities to students.

What will you do on weekends? Visit friends, go shopping, attend a party or play online games? Perhaps all these weekend activities are out of vogue. You can join several people who find weekend jobs to spend their weekends.

CHAPTER 6: EARN $1,000 IN JUST ONE WEEKEND.

We've all seen the headlines on the front of magazines at the grocery store claiming that it's easy to earn outrageous amounts of money in no or little time. And you've likely visited other websites in your quest to make more money, websites depicting a luxurious mansion and exotic sports cars in the driveway to create the idea of effortless wealth.

I've purchased the magazines, read the articles, and purchased quite a few of these online programs. They all seem to tell you just enough to meet the letter of the law, but they never tell you everything you need to know to earn the amount of money they claim you can make, which is extremely frustrating.

I wish, for once, that someone would tell me "how" to do it! Clarify it for me! Please simplify it so I can comprehend it!

So that is what I shall do. I will demonstrate how it is feasible to earn $1,000 in a single weekend.

So, let's get started.

This begins with selling. Don't claim that you can't sell. I am confident that you can. You sell yourself when you apply for a job, don't you? Although this chapter is about selling, it isn't the type you can expect. People will already recognize that they want and need what you're selling, so you won't need to convince them to purchase it. There is very little selling to be done.

If you can approach an unfamiliar person and say, "Hello. How are you?" it is ok.

Second, money is required to make money. It would be best if you had something to sell, as there will be an investment, but the initial investment need not be hundreds of dollars. I began with barely $200. (I recognize that even $200 is money for some people; I used to feel the same way.) Some individuals begin with significantly less.) but it's tough to make money without spending it first, isn't it?

Third, I exclusively deal with brand-new items. I don't trawl through thrift stores, attend garage and yard sales searching for items to resell or dive into dumpsters.

So what do I do? I sell at flea markets. I've been doing this for decades and have made a decent living working weekends alone. (I joke with my pals that my weekends last five days!)

There is no rocket science involved. I purchase products at wholesale costs, and UPS delivers them to me. I bring them to the flea market on Saturday morning and exhibit them on my tables in an attractive manner.

When customers arrive, I greet them with a pleasant "Good morning!" and begin a discussion as if

I had known them for years. I might compliment them on their clothing color or something like that. Everyone enjoys compliments.

They will approach my tables to examine my wares when they observe my friendliness. I will monitor their gaze as closely as possible to determine their interest and describe the item's benefits - what it can do for them, how it can make their lives easier or better, etc.

This is less about marketing and more about being helpful. Simply smile and be cordial.

Before you know it, they are picking up items, examining them closely, and deciding for themselves whether they are worth the price I have set. It is the case, and a further sale is made.

I maintain reasonable prices. Yes, I mark them up to make a respectable profit, but I retain my prices below retail. Customers know what other retailers charge for similar things and adore a good deal.

I put up at the largest, busiest flea markets, where anywhere from 1,000 to 5,000 customers will pass by my booth daily. A percentage of those individuals will stop and look, and a percentage of those who stop and look will make a purchase.

$1,000 per weekend equals $500 per day (two-day weekend). Approximately 33%, or $165, of the $500 in revenue is consumed by expenses (space rental and your wholesale cost of the items + delivery). To earn $500 daily, I must make approximately $665 in daily sales. I often surpass that.

To be completely transparent, I don't have only $200 worth of items available. I have between $1,500 and $2,000 worth of goods (at my wholesale cost). I started my business with only $200 because that was all I could afford, and I reinvested the proceeds by purchasing more items and increasing my business. I earned $800 in a single day in just a few months.

I mark up my products by around three times their wholesale price. If I paid $1 for an item, I would sell it for $3 to $4. If I paid $10 for it, I charge $30 to $40 for it. Most customers purchase multiple items while they are there. I easily make many hundred sales per day.

Therefore. Is this wishful thinking? No.

Does it work? Yes!

Can you do it?

I believe you already know the response.

In this day and age, many individuals need weekend employment. Aim for one that pays well and can make your weekend more enjoyable rather than dreary.

CHAPTER 7: STEPS TO FIND A WEEKEND JOB QUICKLY.

Life is unpredictable, and you can need weekend or part-time employment quickly. Here are seven steps that consistently result in weekend employment in the shortest time.

Step 1: identify your interests and strengths.

You can be thinking, but the position is part-time! True. However, many part-time jobs have turned full-time when they coincide with what inspires or is a strength of the individual.

Moreover, why waste your weekends doing something you dislike when you have alternatives? Do a fast inventory of your hobbies, strengths, and what you're truly good at, and you are on your way to finding a great job.

Step 2: Prepare.

Preparation involves a resume and other details, such as having voice mail to ensure someone can reach you. Your CV need not be extensive but should highlight your most relevant skills and experiences and appeal to folks who share your interests and abilities.

Preparation entails having reference information, prior and current employment information, and other information that a potential weekend employer may need in a hurry readily available.

Also, determine beforehand the type of work you desire, definitely won't accept and why, the hours you are prepared to sacrifice, the distance you are willing to drive for weekend employment, and any other limitations. Distinguish the desirable from the non-negotiable, and be aware of why you've established such rigid boundaries. Protect your perimeter.

Step 3: Submit an Application Online.

Search part-time work sites and submit applications for all relevant positions.

Step 4: Apply Face-to-Face.

After you've applied to online opportunities, you should start knocking on doors. This necessitates walking the mall and asking every potential client if they are hiring. I understand that this may feel weird, but how you think makes no difference. I'm amazed by the number of part-time changes resulting from the question, "Are you seeking weekend or part-time work?" Sometimes it's that straightforward.

Step 5: Build Your Network.

Inform your social network that you are seeking a weekend or part-time job and the type of work you like. Most positions are not publicized, and most firms prefer to acquire staff fast, particularly for part-time work. This implies they want to rely on employee referrals, making it all the more vital that you inform their network of your demands. They will assist you.

Step 6: Keep Account.

Keep track of who you've spoken with, particularly if you need to contact them again. Success lies in the follow-up. Often, they may not have an immediate opening, but if they ask you to check back, make a note of it and do so and you will be distinct from the crowd. Keep records so that your second follow-up is more effective.

Step 7: Increase Your Choices.

If you haven't found a weekend or part-time job yet, you can need to seek work-at-home options. There are legitimate data entry, home assembly, writing, and other work-at-home opportunities. Avoid occupations that sound too good or don't utilize your unique skills and abilities.

CHAPTER 8; MY TOP 50 WAYS TO MAKE $100 ONLINE ON A WEEKEND.

You can earn $100 online in one or two days on the weekend, provided you take the appropriate steps. Here are 50 ways to achieve this and make a constant stream of other part-time income.

1. Create a free ebook on a trending subject and upsell your customers to a premium offering. Distribute it online for free.

2. Create a review of a popular product or book, post it on your blog or website with an affiliate link and distribute your piece on a huge number of social networking and other websites.

3. If you already have an email list, you can send an email promoting a new product to you or

someone else as part of an email with valuable content.

4. Write three to five outstanding articles for examiner.com and promote them.

5. Publish multiple fresh blog entries with Google AdSense and distribute them on Twitter, Facebook, and other social networking and bookmarking sites. Make them topical, pertinent, and engaging.

6. Create a few video reviews of popular books or other products and advertise them with an affiliate link on multiple video-sharing websites.

7. Create a hot offer and a hot piece of content, then share the content with a link to the hot offer on Facebook.

8. Use Twitter's search function to locate people looking for a solution to a problem and either design a product that answers their problem or offers an affiliate product.

9. Offer a product that addresses an issue or answers a pressing topic that people are asking on message boards and forums.

10. Visit Facebook groups and perform the same actions as in numbers 8 and 9.

11. Create a brief eBay auction for a popular product and sell it.

12. Distribute a free ebook, including affiliate links, and urge individuals to spread it.

13. Host an internet party and sell certain things in high demand.

14. Charge a fee for participation in a teleseminar on a popular topic.

15. Charge a fee for participating in a hot topic webinar.

16. Promote a website-wide product clearance offer to the entire world.

17. Create an online video series on a trending subject. Give one away for free and sell the others.

18. Spend the entire day conducting paid surveys.

19. Create a single-page website with valuable information and include a PayPal donation button, requesting that visitors contribute whatever they deem your content worthwhile.

20. Take some adorable and sophisticated photographs. Post your pictures on Facebook or another popular website and offer visitors the opportunity to purchase prints.

21. Upload some one-of-a-kind t-shirts, stickers, and other products to Café Press and market your website aggressively.

22. Create some high-quality logos and make them available for purchase.

23. Create a paid audio series similar to a podcast and sell it.

24. Find a business that needs a video advertisement. Create the advertisement and post it online on their behalf.

25. Find a business that needs a website and develop it for them.

26. Offer to produce internet video testimonials for a few firms. Charge them for this service.

27. Find a client needing a freelance writer and spend your time creating articles for them.

28. You can sell advertising space on your website with sufficient traffic.

29. Find a website that needs to sell some ads and request a revenue share. Then, contact

prospective buyers and propose the sale of the advertising.

30. Find a few companies willing to pay you to help review their products on your blog.

31. Offer to write blog posts for someone in exchange for compensation.

32. Find the best-selling books on Amazon and make textual and video advertisements with your affiliate link.

33. Offer to speak as a guest on a teleseminar and fee for your expertise.

34. Offer to appear on a live TV broadcast about a subject in which you have expertise and request payment.

35. Plan a live event on a trending topic and sell tickets online.

36. Combine some of your best content into an informational product, sell it for a ridiculously low price and promote it aggressively.

37. Offer to prepare delicious, easy-to-prepare meals for folks, then advertise them online in your local region and deliver them.

38. Run a contest for a few hours in which individuals can win high-value, popular goods and offer those who did not win a substantial discount on the product.

39. Offer to write and mail greeting cards or postcards for a small business or person who needs many cards or postcards sent.

40. Advertise that you can perform local courier services for a few individuals.

41. Find multiple subjects you can write about on Associated Content and compose the corresponding articles.

42. Offer your services as a weekend virtual assistant to a firm needing minimal internetwork.

43. Advertise that you can conduct weekend typing from home for one or two clients.

44. Visit upwork.com and search for jobs you can successfully bid on and complete.

45. If you speak a foreign language, you can discover someone who needs translation work online.

46. Take photographs of some adorable animals and sell the images online with the owners' permission.

47. Create and sell some original PLR material.

48. Create gift baskets and sell them alongside your other products or as a weekend-only promotion.

49. Find a business that needs help setting up its social networking pages and do it for them.

50. Charge people to attend a virtual lecture or conference that targets a specific niche.

CONCLUSION.

Today, everyone is seeking extra cash. If you are in school or employed in an office, you will only have time to earn extra money on the weekends. Be an entrepreneur on the weekends and make other money.

There are many opportunities to make money on the weekends if you are resourceful enough. Different weekend employment opportunities are available for those looking to earn extra cash on the weekends.

If you have a computer and an internet connection, you can first consider working from home and earning money. The Internet is one of the largest marketplaces in the world. Using the internet's resources, there is no limit to how much can be earned.

Before starting, you must conduct extensive research to determine your area of interest and the field that would fit best with your available time and work schedule.

You can even do this twice every week to earn extra money. Many periodicals and newspapers are continuously seeking weekend delivery personnel. Newspaper delivery could be another option to consider. You can discover relevant information in your local newspaper.

If you have a passion for gardening, you might also consider being a weekend landscaper. Plant trees, tidy and mow lawns and enjoy your hobby while making other money. Surely, your neighbors are looking for someone like you.

You need motivation, initiative, and zeal to be a successful entrepreneur. The dollars are a natural consequence. Be an entrepreneur on the weekends and earn other money.

Try what I did if you need money immediately or within the hour. I am making more money today than I did in my previous business, and you can, too, if you click the link below and read the incredible true tale. I was suspicious for only ten seconds after joining before I knew what this was. You will also be beaming from ear to ear, as I was.

As you can see, there are many options for mothers to earn a reasonable livelihood by working simply on weekends. Most people don't realize that a weekend business can be expanded to where you will never need another 9-to-5 job again. If you are still unsure about these methods of making money, you should know that many other options are available.

You must first have everything set up properly. This necessitates providing your home office with the necessary equipment, including a computer and comfortable home office chairs. You must realize that to earn money online.

Management Skills for Managers.

1. Time Management for Managers
2. Employee Coaching for Managers
3. Team Building for Managers
4. Self Confidence for Managers
5. Negotiation Skills for Managers
6. Customer Service Skills for Managers
7. Assertiveness for Managers
8. Business Etiquette for Managers
9. Listening Skills for Managers
10. Leadership Skills for Managers
11. Communication Skills for Managers
12. Presentation Skills for Managers
13. Stress Management for Managers
14. Decision Making for Managers
15. Conflict Management for Managers.

Series: Financial Freedom at Any Age.

- Achieving Financial Freedom in your 20's
- Achieving Financial Freedom in your 30's
- Achieving Financial Freedom in your 40's
- Achieving Financial Freedom in your 50's
- Achieving Financial Freedom in your 60's
- Achieving Financial Freedom in your 70's and beyond.
- Achieving Financial Freedom in children
- Achieving Financial Freedom in teenagers
- Achieving Financial Freedom in college students.
- Financial Scams to be Aware of in Retirement.

Series: Personal Finance for You.
- ➤ Buying and Selling Crypto for Beginners
- ➤ Why Investing in Dividend Stocks Makes Sense.

Series: Wealth 2022.

- ➤ Online Entrepreneurship.
- ➤ Starting Your Own Business
- ➤ Wealth Management
- ➤ Passive Income.
- ➤ 12 Steps to Starting your own business.

Series: Excellent Customer Service

- ➤ Excellent Customer Service in Retail
- ➤ Excellent Customer Service in Fast Food
- ➤ Excellent Customer Service in Full-Service Restaurant
- ➤ Excellent Customer Service in Teaching.
- ➤ Excellent Customer Service in Real Estate
- ➤ Excellent Customer Service in a Call Center
- ➤ Excellent Customer Service as a Receptionist
- ➤ Excellent Customer Service in a Hotel
- ➤ Excellent Customer Service in Selling
- ➤ Excellent Customer Service No Matter the Situation.

- Excellent Customer Service in Dental Office
- Excellent Customer Service in Medical Office.

Series: Quick Money.

- Quick Money in a Week
- Quick Money in a Weekend
- Quick Money in a Month
- Quick Money for Students.

Series: How to Promote

- How to Make your Business Thrive During a Recession
- How to Promote your Recipe Book
- How to Promote your Children Book.

Author Bio

D.K. Hawkins. D.K. enjoys reading personal business books as well as spending time outdoors. More books will come in this collection, so please follow on Amazon for more books.

Thank you for your purchase of this book.

I honestly do appreciate it and appreciate you, my excellent customer.

God Bless You.

D.K. Hawkins.